# Jacinta's Story

# Jacinta's Story

THE STORY OF THE APPARITIONS
OF FATIMA AS RETOLD AND
ILLUSTRATED

by
Andrea Fragelli

The Story of the Apparitions of Fatima
as imaginatively told by Jacinta Marto.
A project of the
**America Needs Fatima Campaign**
Text and illustrations by Andrea Fragelli
Copyright © 1996 by The American Society for the
Defense of Tradition, Family and Property (TFP)
P .O. Box 1868, York, Pennsylvania 17405

Library of Congress Catalog Card Number 96-86158
ISBN # 1-877905-32-1
Printed in the United States of America

YOUR CHILD'S LIBRARY OF INNOCENCE

*To Our Lady of Fatima,*
*the light of my life,*
*my guiding star—my Mother.*

# My name is Jacinta.

I am a child like you, but now I live in Heaven. From here I can see you, and I even know your name. Knowing that you like stories, I want to tell you mine. It's a beautiful story! It happened not only to me but also to my brother Francisco and my cousin Lúcia. We were three shepherd children who thought only of our sheep and our games...until one day the Queen of Heaven visited us. After that visit, things were never the same again—for us or for the world.

I was born in a country called Portugal. It's a small land on the continent of Europe across the great Atlantic Ocean. Let me tell you a bit about my country's history. Then it will be easier for you to understand why the Queen of Heaven came to visit us.

Portugal is small, but only in size. It had a big soul and did many great things for God. And Our Lord had great plans for it.

Around the year 1100 there was a great warrior and nobleman called Alfonso Henriques. He spent his life fighting to make that land independent. One day, while resting in his tent before a great battle, he had a wonderful dream. In his dream, a holy old man came to visit him. Just then, his page awoke him:

"Don Alfonso, Don Alfonso! There is a holy old man who wishes to see you, Sir. He says it is very important." "Send him in, good page," said Don Alfonso as he sat up in his cot.

When the old man came in, Don Alfonso was startled. It was the man in his dream! After a few words of greeting, the old man introduced himself.

"I live as a hermit near by. For many years, I have served our sovereign and heavenly Lord, Jesus Christ. Don Alfonso, you have a good heart, and because of this, my Lord Jesus would like to speak to you. Tonight, when you hear the bell of my hermitage ring, leave your camp and wait for Him."

You may well imagine Don Alfonso's awe at this message. The King of Heaven and Earth wished to speak with him! It could only mean that His Divine Majesty had a very important message for him.

When the bell rang, Don Alfonso Henriques left his camp and waited.

Suddenly, a bright ray of light shone in the night. In the center of the light he saw Jesus Crucified. From the cross Jesus spoke to him; "Alfonso, I am appearing to you not to increase your faith but to strengthen your heart. I want Portugal to be a kingdom, and you to be its king. I also want Portugal to carry the Catholic Faith to many other lands. So that your descendants may know that I gave them this kingdom, your flag shall have five shields on it representing My five wounds."

Thus, the five wounds of Our Lord and Savior became the mark of Portugal, and Alfonso Henriques became its first king. This flag remains the same today as it was then.

Such was the origin of the kingdom of Portugal—a country born from a special wish of Our Lord Jesus Christ!

# The Kingdom of Portugal

# Nuno Alvares

**M**any, many years later, Portugal was being ruled by a bad queen. Her name was Leonor. The Portuguese people did not like Queen Leonor because she wanted to give Portugal to the King of Spain.

But, the King of Heaven did not want this to happen. Our Lord chose a good warrior to fight for Portugal. This man was Nuno Alvares Pereira. He was only twenty-four years old.

Don Nuno was very pious but also very brave. He knew God did not wish Portugal to be given to Spain. Don Nuno disagreed with Queen Leonor and her Spanish friends.

The king of Spain thought Portugal was almost his. He came to Portugal with his army to claim it. But Don Nuno was ready for him! His army was very small compared to the Spanish king's army, but that did not bother him at all. He believed that God was with him, and he was faithful to God. He beat the Spanish army badly in a huge battle.

Now Portugal was free once again!

The new king was Prince John.

Don Nuno became the king's champion. He was the greatest man in Portugal after King John.

When Don Nuno grew old, he gave up this great honor and became a simple monk. His job was to watch the gates of his monastery.

When his friends saw him at such a humble job, they exclaimed, "Don Nuno, how can you be guarding a gate? You were once the king's own champion!"

The holy man answered simply, "My lords, my lords, in God's house everything is so great that even little things are very big."

And his old men-at-arms were in awe. They said, "He is a great knight, but he is an even greater saint!"

Don Nuno asked the abbot of the monastery for only one favor: He wanted to wear his beloved armor under his habit. To this day, he is venerated as Blessed Nuno Alvares, Portugal's great champion and saint.

# The Caravels

The years went by. In 1450, a prince, Henry, began teaching men how to build better ships. He wanted them to look for new lands for Our Lord and for the king. All Portugal worked and prayed for these adventures.

The ships were beautiful and a great symbol of my country.

They seemed to say, "I am small but my soul is great, for it is full of faith. The sea does not frighten me. My sails carry Our Lord's symbol. He once said, 'Be calm,' and the sea became calm. Another time, He said, 'Be still,' and the winds became still."

Portugal's proud caravels found many new lands and seas. One of the great lands the Portuguese discovered is now the huge country of Brazil. It is so big that twenty Portugals could easily fit into it! And thus Portugal became a great and powerful empire, just as Our Lord had promised Don Alfonso Henriques.

You see that my country was always very dear to Our Lord! It showed its love and gratitude for Him in many, many ways. But, unfortunately, many times it did not behave very well. Sometimes, Portugal forgot about its many blessings and was ungrateful.

However, Our Lord never forgot Portugal. He remembered what its great men and saints had done for Him. Once again, He chose to bless my country with a great message. This time, He sent the message through His beloved Mother, the Queen of Heaven and Earth.

This is where my story begins. This time, Our Lady did not come to a king or to a great warrior. Instead, she appeared to three little shepherd children. I was one of them.

# The Angel o*

**M**y full name is Jacinta Marto. I lived in Aljustrel, not far from Lisbon. Lisbon is the most important city in Portugal.

The name Aljustrel has a musical ring, doesn't it? Until today it is a very, very small village surrounded by fields and olive trees. I lived there with my father and mother and ten brothers and sisters. My house was small but neat. I loved my brother Francisco the best. He was two years older than I.

Just a short way down the road from us lived my cousin, Lúcia dos Santos and her family. She was a year older than Francisco. The three of us always played together. We took our family's sheep to pasture every day in the fields surrounding Aljustrel. The sheep ate grass, and we played. Sometimes we prayed.

We did not pray very well. Our parents had taught us to pray the Rosary because this pleased the Blessed Mother very much. We would take out our rosaries and on the large beads we would simply say, "Our Father"—and nothing more. On the Hail Mary beads we were much quicker. As we slipped each bead through our fingers we repeated, "Hail Mary-Holy Mary, Hail Mary-Holy Mary, Hail Mary-Holy Mary..." Later, we learned to pray the Rosary properly.

We had a favorite spot for our games called Loca do Cabeço. We had lots of fun jumping over its rocks. The view from the top of this place was very beautiful. We could see the valley below and some of the houses in Aljustrel.

Portugal

Fear not, I am the Angel of Peace. Pray with me.

One beautiful day in the year 1916, as we were playing, a sudden strong wind shook the trees. Surprised, we looked up, for it was a very calm day. Then, over the valley towards the East, we began to see a light high above the trees. The light, whiter than snow, surrounded the shining form of a young man! He seemed more brilliant than a crystal struck by the rays of the sun! As he came nearer we could see him better. He was young, about fourteen or fifteen years old, and very handsome. We were so surprised that we did not move. We could not say a single word.

Coming very close, he said, "Fear not, I am the Angel of Peace. Pray with me."

He knelt down and bowed low until his forehead touched the ground. We did the same and repeated the words we heard him say: "**My God, I believe, I adore, I hope, and I love Thee. I beg Thee forgiveness for those who do not believe, do not adore, do not hope, and do not love Thee.**"

After he had said this prayer twice, he rose and told us to pray it often because Our Lord and Our Lady were listening to us from heaven. Then he disappeared.

After he left, we stayed on our knees for a long time with our foreheads touching the ground. We repeated the beautiful prayer the angel had taught us over and over. We felt so full of God that we dared not speak to each other. The next day we still felt as if God had touched us. We did not tell anyone about the angel.

Another day, when we were playing at Lúcia's house, the angel suddenly appeared again.

"What are you doing?" he asked. "Pray, pray a great deal! The Sacred Heart of Jesus and the Immaculate Heart of Mary have merciful plans for you. Offer prayers and sacrifices all the time to the Most High."

Lúcia asked him what he meant. He explained that we should offer God some sacrifice, something that was a bit difficult for us to do. He said we should do this to console God for the many sins that people commit and to save sinners from Hell. He told us he was our country's guardian angel—the Angel of Portugal. Then he disappeared.

The "Angel of Portugal"! That sounded beautiful to us! We knew each of us had a Guardian Angel, but we did not know that countries have angels too. Wow! We had met the Guardian Angel of Portugal!

Later that same summer we saw that beautiful angel for the last time. We were kneeling with our foreheads to the ground and saying the first prayer the angel had taught us. We sensed a great light over us. Looking up, we saw the Angel of Portugal holding a golden chalice in his left hand. Above the chalice was a host. Drops of blood fell from it into the cup.

Leaving the chalice and the host suspended in mid air, the angel bent low beside us and taught us another prayer: "**Most Holy Trinity, Father, Son, and Holy Ghost, I adore Thee profoundly and offer Thee the most precious Body, Blood,**

Soul, and Divinity of Jesus Christ, present in all the tabernacles of the earth, in reparation for the insults, sacrileges, and indifference with which He is offended. And through the infinite merits of His most Sacred Heart and of the Immaculate Heart of Mary, I beg Thee for the conversion of poor sinners."

Getting up, he again took the chalice and the host in his hand. He gave the host to Lúcia. Francisco and I wondered if he would offer us Holy Communion as we had not made our First Communion. He leaned toward us and had us drink from the chalice. After this, he again knelt and repeated with us the same prayer three times. "Most Holy Trinity...." Then he disappeared. We never saw him again.

From that day on, we did everything the Angel had taught us. We began to pray better and more seriously than before. The great Angel of Peace had come to prepare us for a greater visitor.

# Lady More Br...

It had been six months since the Angel appeared to us. It was spring, May 13, 1917. That day we took our sheep to a small property belonging to Lúcia's parents. It was called the Cova da Iria.

The day was clear and we were playing. Suddenly, we saw two flashes like lightning in the sky. As we looked in that direction, we saw over a small oak tree a lady dressed all in white! She seemed more brilliant than the sun! The light around her was clearer and stronger than that of the angel. And her face, oh, her face! It was very, very beautiful! It was neither sad nor happy, but serious. Her hands were joined together as if she were praying. A rosary hung from her right hand. Her clothes seemed to be made of light. Her dress and veil were white, but her veil was edged with gold.

Without really knowing what we were doing, we approached the small tree. We were so close to her that the light around her also encircled us. Francisco could see the lady very well, but only Lúcia and I were able to hear and see her.

"Do not be afraid, I will not harm you," she said.

"Where is Your Grace from?" asked my cousin Lúcia.

"I am from heaven," answered the lady, pointing to the sky.

"And what does Your Grace wish of me?"

"I have come to ask you to come here for six months, on the thirteenth day of each month at this same hour. Later, I shall tell you who I am and what I want."

"And will I go to heaven?"
asked Lúcia.

"Yes, you will."

"And Jacinta?"

"Also."

"And Francisco?"

"Also, but he must say
many rosaries!"

The beautiful lady asked us if we would like to help save poor sinners. Lucia answered, "Yes."

The lady said, "Then you will have much to suffer. But God will help you."

As she said this, she opened her hands. Strong light flowed from them, penetrating our hearts and souls. We felt very close to God and had never felt so happy. Suddenly we wanted to pray! We knelt down and repeated to ourselves, "O Most Holy Trinity, I adore Thee! My God, my God, I love Thee in the Most Blessed Sacrament."

A moment later the lady added, "Pray the Rosary every day to obtain peace for the world and to end the war." You see, Europe had been in an awful war for three years. It was the First World War.

Then the lady slowly began to rise toward the East and disappeared in the distance.

## At Home

Francisco and I told our family about the lady. They did not believe us. Lúcia's mother thought she was lying and punished her. Lúcia was truly honest and never lied in her life, so she was very hurt by her mother's punishment.

Both of our mothers were so worried that they took us to the parish priest. He was very kind to us and asked us some questions. Then he told our mothers not to worry and not to punish us anymore. He thought that maybe we were just imagining things.

So our mothers decided to pretend that nothing had happened. They hoped we would forget about it. But how could we forget the beautiful lady? The opposite happened. We spoke and thought of the beautiful lady all the time and could not wait to see her again on June 13.

A short while before we were supposed to return to Cova da Iria,

Lúcia surprised Francisco and I by saying that she would not be going with us to meet the lady.

"June 13 is the feast of our Portuguese saint, Saint Anthony, and I am going to the fair with Mother," she said.

"Lúcia," we protested, "how can you not go to the Cova? You promised the lady that you would!"

"No, you two go, but I must go with my mother."

"But, why?!"

"Well, Mother has been saying that perhaps... perhaps... it is the devil who is appearing to us disguised as the beautiful lady..."

At this, I began to cry. I could not believe that such a beautiful person could be a devil. Nor could I think of going without Lúcia.

"How can you say such a thing, Lúcia?" I asked in tears. "The devil is a horrible and ugly thing. He could never appear so lovely and brilliant as the lady we saw!"

Francisco quickly added, "How can we go without you? The lady speaks to you, not to us. I cannot even hear her."

But Lúcia would not change her mind. She was determined to go to the fair.

# The Lady's Second Visit

June 13 dawned. Francisco and I were afraid to go without our elder cousin. So we sat alone at home. Our entire family had gone to the fair. You can imagine our joy and relief when we saw Lúcia coming towards us! She had changed her mind!

We left quickly for the Cova da Iria to see the lady. But this time, we were not alone. Our story had spread, and at least fifty people were there.

They wanted to see for themselves what had been happening at the Cova.

As we waited, we knelt and began to say our Rosary. We had said five decades and still she was not there. We were about to begin another when Lúcia exclaimed, "Here she is!"

Just like the first time, there was a flash of light and the lady appeared standing over the holm oak, just above us. Only Lúcia spoke.

"What does Your Grace wish of me?"

"I want you to come here on the thirteenth of next month, to pray the Rosary every day, and to learn to read. Later, I shall say what I want."

Then Lúcia asked her to cure a sick acquaintance. The lady said that if the person converted she would cure him during the year.

Lúcia then said, "I would like to ask you to take us to heaven."

"Yes, I shall take Jacinta and Francisco soon, but you will remain here

for some time yet. Jesus wants you to make me known and loved. He wishes to establish devotion to my Immaculate Heart in the world. I promise salvation to those who practice this devotion. Those souls will be loved by God like flowers arranged by me to decorate His throne."

"Will I stay here alone?" asked Lúcia.

"No, daughter. Does that make you suffer much? Do not be sad. I will never forget you. My Immaculate Heart will be your refuge and the road that will lead you to God."

On saying this, she opened her hands as she had done the first time. Again we felt pierced by that brilliant light and we were filled with happiness and devotion. Next to her hand was a heart surrounded by thorns that seemed to pierce it. We understood that it was her Immaculate Heart, so hurt by people's sins.

The lady then slowly began to rise and glide towards the East until she disappeared again.

The people were now talking all around us. Most of them did not believe we had seen anything and thought we were lying. They pressed around us with questions, even insults. But a few persons noticed something strange about the holm oak; the small buds at the very top of the tree were facing upward. They seemed to have been brushed by the lady's dress as she rose to heaven.

Lúcia, Francisco, and I slipped away from the crowd and went home.

By now our lives had really changed! We counted the days until the lady came again. We were also praying much better. Above all, we no longer rushed through our Rosary. Anything that made us suffer, we offered to God to make up for the many people who hurt Him by sinning.

# A Terrible Vision

July 13 finally came! It was to be our third meeting with the heavenly lady! At twelve o'clock we were waiting at the usual place. This time there were about five thousand people waiting with us.

As the moment came for the lady to appear, my father and others noticed the sun grow dim. A breeze cooled the hot summer air. A small grayish cloud appeared over the holm oak.

Finally, we saw the usual flash of light and the lady appeared as beautiful and brilliant as the midday sun!

As usual, Lúcia began the conversation. "What does Your Grace wish?"

And the lady answered in her beautiful voice, "I want

"You saw Hell, where the souls of poor sinners go."

you to come here on the thirteenth of next month and to continue praying the Rosary every day in honor of Our Lady of the Rosary to obtain peace for the world and the end of the war, for she alone can help."

Lúcia: "I would like to ask you to tell us who you are and to perform a miracle so everyone will believe that Your Grace appears to us."

The lady: "Continue to come here every month. In October, I will tell you who I am and what I wish, and I will perform a miracle so that everyone may believe."

Then Lucia asked her to cure some sick people and also to make some bad people become good. The lady answered that if they prayed the Rosary all the time, they would receive these favors that year.

Then she said, "Sacrifice yourselves for sinners, and say many times, especially when you make some sacrifice, 'O Jesus, this is for love of Thee, for the conversion of sinners, and in reparation for the sins committed against the Immaculate Heart of Mary.'"

As she said this, she opened her hands as she had done the two previous times. The rays streaming from them opened the earth. Before us we saw an ocean of fire! There were horrible devils and the souls of people floating around like red-hot coals. There were so many of them! They seemed to be thrown about in the flames, falling everywhere like a shower of sparks. There were terrible cries of despair. The devils stood out like horrible and unknown animals with disgusting shapes.

We were very much afraid! If it had not been for the lady's promise to take us to heaven we would have died of fright. We had seen Hell.

She knew how terrified we were for she only let us see this for an instant. When she took the vision away, we raised our frightened eyes to her. Looking at us full of kindness and sadness, she said, "You saw Hell, where the souls of poor sinners go. To save them, God wishes to establish devotion to my Immaculate Heart in the world. If they do what I shall tell you, many souls will be saved and there will be peace."

She then told us that the terrible war in Europe was going to end. But she also said that if people did not stop offending God, another even worse war would come. To keep this next war from coming she said that the country of Russia should be especially offered to her Immaculate Heart. She also said that people should receive Holy Communion on the first Saturday of each month for five months in a row. If what she asked was done, she said that Russia would convert. If not, Russia would spread its evils all around the world. In consequence, terrible things would happen to many people and nations. The Pope, too, would suffer very much.

# HOW TO PRAY THE ROSARY

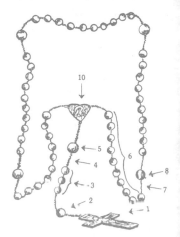

1. Make the Sign of the Cross and say the "Apostles Creed."

2. Say the "Our Father."

3. Say three "Hail Marys."

4. Say the "Glory be to the Father."

5. Announce the First Mystery; then say the "Our Father."

6. Say ten "Hail Marys," while meditating on the Mystery.

7. Say the "Glory be to the Father."

8. After each decade say the following prayer requested by the Blessed Virgin Mary at Fatima: "O my Jesus, forgive us our sins, save us from the fires of hell, lead all souls to Heaven, especially those who have most need of your mercy."

9. Announce the Second Mystery: then say the "Our Father." Repeat 6, 7 and 8 and continue with the Third, Fourth and Fifth Mysteries in the same manner.

10. Say the 'Hail, Holy Queen' after the five decades are completed.

11. As a general rule, the Joyful Mysteries are said on Monday and Thursday; the Sorrowful Mysteries on Tuesday and Friday; the Glorious Mysteries on Wednesday and Saturday. Depending on the Season, each of the Mysteries is recommended for Sunday.

Marians of the Immaculate Conception
ASSOCIATION OF MARIAN HELPERS
STOCKBRIDGE, MA 01263-0004

Prayer Line: 1-800-804-3823
Order Line: 1-800-462-7426
Website: www.marian.org

# Pray
# The Rosary
# Daily

Then she added, "In the end, my Immaculate Heart will triumph. The Holy Father will consecrate Russia to me, and a certain period of peace will be granted to the world. Russia will be converted."

Then she made a beautiful promise about my country. "In Portugal, the Faith will always be kept."

Always looking kindly at Lúcia, she continued, "Do not tell anyone but Francisco about this.

She also told us another secret, but this one we could not tell at all—not ever.

The lady then said again, "When you pray the Rosary, after each decade, say, **'O my Jesus, forgive us, save us from the fire of hell; lead all souls to heaven, especially those in most need.'"**

Lucia asked, "Does Your Grace wish anything else of me?"

"No," answered the lady, "today I do not wish anything else of you."

As always, she rose toward the East and disappeared into the blue sky. This time, we heard a sound like thunder; the visit was over.

We were so scared by the vision of Hell! We could not forget it. People would not leave us alone.

"What did the lady say this time?" they asked.

"It's a secret. We cannot tell," we replied, over and over.

Some people believed us, but many did not. They made fun of us and called us liars. All this hurt very much. But what did it matter? We had seen Hell and the enormous number of people who go there and never come out!

By now, every chance we had, we gladly offered sacrifices for poor sinners. We did not complain any more when life was hard. We offered everything up to God so souls could go to Heaven. We also wanted to console that beautiful Heart of Mary we had seen in the lady's hand.

Poor Lúcia suffered the most after these visits. Her mother was very, very strict and was upset that her daughter was fooling so many people. Lúcia was often punished, and her brothers and sisters made fun of her. But she offered all this up as a sacrifice to God. Francisco and I did everything we could to help her.

When we took our sheep out to graze, we talked a lot about all we had seen and heard. Some things we did not understand, such as what the lady had said about Russia.

"Russia must be a wicked country," said Francisco, "for the lady to say that if it is not offered to her Immaculate Heart it will spread its evil ways throughout the world and destroy many nations."

"It doesn't sound like a very good place," I replied. "Very few people there must ever say the Rosary."

But a few months later we understood what the Lady meant. Some evil people took over Russia. They were called "communists." Communists are people who hate God and everything good. They killed Russia's king, the queen, and their children. They made the Russian people miserable and began to spread their evil ideas all over the world.

We decided that God needed more sacrifices. We wanted to console Our Lord for all this wickedness. We understood that all these things make Him very sad, just as when children are bad and make their parents very sad.

So, we said our Rosaries every day as the lady had asked us to do. We offered as many sacrifices as we could. One day, we gave our lunches to some poor children. On another, we did not drink any water. Another day, we found some very rough rope. We got the idea of tying pieces of it around our waists until they hurt. We kept remembering those souls screaming in Hell, and we wanted to stop sinners from going there.

You see, dear friend, you can also make little sacrifices. I don't mean that you have to give your lunches away or wear rough cords. But, when you have something on your plate you don't like very much, eat it without complaining. This will do two things: it will make your soul stronger and it will help keep a poor sinner from going to Hell. Isn't that worth it?

When you feel like hitting your brother or sister for something unkind they said, hold your temper and don't hit them. By doing this, you will hit the devil instead and will take a soul away from his mean claws.

There are so many small things like this that you can do. Above all, Jesus and the Blessed Virgin will be very pleased, as They were pleased with us.

# Kidnapped

After July 13, the news that we were seeing "a heavenly lady" spread like wildfire. Our story was in the newspapers all over Portugal. Some people who did not believe in God were very angry.

One of these people was the mayor of the largest town in our area, the town of Ourem. Oh, he was very upset!

"What is this about children seeing a heavenly lady? What do they mean? Do you people really believe in heavenly beings? It is about time we stop believing in such nonsense! And now I hear there were more than five thousand people there last time! Ridiculous! Pretty soon the entire country will go to Fátima to see this lady! I must put an end to this NOW!"

The mayor of Ourem was a very cunning man. He came up with a mean plan.

On August 13, we were ready to go to the Cova da Iria to meet our beautiful lady for the fourth time. As we were about to leave, a big shiny black car pulled up to our door. Who do you think stepped out but the mayor of Ourem! He politely asked our parents to let him take us to the Cova in his car. Everyone was impressed. You see, at that time, cars were a rare sight. Our parents said yes, so we got into the car. But to tell you the truth, we were scared.

The mayor drove out of our village. We soon knew that something was wrong. Lúcia spoke up, "Please, sir, we are going the wrong way. Cova da Iria is behind us."

"I just thought we would take a little trip to Ourem first," said the mayor, "I want you to speak to a priest there."

Francisco was alarmed. "To Ourem? But we don't have time. The lady comes at twelve o'clock. We are going to be late!"

"Have you forgotten, young man, how much faster cars are than donkey carts?" replied the mayor. "We will be to Ourem and back in no time."

That calmed us down a little, but we were still anxious. On reaching Ourem the car sped right past the church and the priest's house. We were not going there either. We finally stopped in front of a huge building.

The mayor turned to us. He had a very mean look on his face and an ugly glint in his eyes.

"You are very stubborn and untruthful children.

With your lies about a 'heavenly lady' at the Cova da Iria, you have caused a great commotion. You deserve to be punished. Either you deny that you have seen anything and tell me your 'secret,' or there is no telling what I will do to you!"

We then entered the building and went through the hallways. Soon we stood in front of a barred door. Inside we saw a group of rough-looking men. Yes, this was the jail of Ourem! The men staring at us from behind the bars were criminals!

The jailer brought the keys and we were pushed into the middle of those men. Of course, we were scared, but we were even more worried. By this time the lady must have come and gone already. And we were not there!

The prisoners jeered: "Why, we've got company!" roared one.

"Since when do they send us babies?" scowled another.

"These are pick-pockets for sure," said a third. "What did you steal, boy?"

Lúcia bravely spoke up. "We are not pick-pockets, sir. We are here because a beautiful lady has been appearing to us at the Cova in Fátima. The mayor says we are lying, but we are not."

The men stared in amazement. What nonsense was this? "You children better not get the mayor angry," said one of the men. "He can get you into lots of trouble if you start making up stories."

"But sir, we didn't make up stories!" I cried.

"That's right," added Francisco, "and even if the mayor locked us up for ever we could never say she didn't visit us, because she did!"

The men began murmuring among themselves. Then I had an idea. It must have been about twelve o'clock. If we could not be at the Cova, we could at least think of the lady and say the Rosary.

I took a medal from around my neck and asked one of the prisoners to hang it up on the wall. He did so. Then, we knelt down and began to pray the Rosary. At first, only our voices were heard; the men were quiet. Suddenly, a few rough voices began to join us in the Hail Marys. Soon, most of them were saying the Rosary with us. The others kept a respectful silence.

After that, they took us more seriously and even made friends with us.

Sometime later the mayor returned. He was sure we would be scared to death and ready to deny everything. Instead, he found us stronger than ever in our faith in the heavenly lady. He was furious! He took us to his own house and locked us up in a room. The room was dreary and we did not know what was going to happen next.

"What will he do to us?" my brother asked Lúcia.

"I don't know," she answered. "Perhaps he will beat us. If he does, we must be ready to offer it to God for poor sinners."

That was a difficult moment! What would happen? The only kind soul in the place was the mayor's wife. She brought us food and something to drink. But when we asked her how long it would be before we could go home, she said it might be several days.

Then I started to cry. I was homesick. We had never been away from our parents and families before. But, we had seen Hell and all those sinners lost forever. The lady had said we would have much to suffer. So we began to repeat the words she had taught us: "O my Jesus, I offer this for love of Thee, for the conversion of sinners, and in reparation for all the wrongs done to the Immaculate Heart of Mary." Then we prayed our Rosary. It was good we did, for we felt a special strength every time we said it.

# Boiling Oil

Lúcia, Francisco, and I had been prisoners for about five days when the mayor suddenly stormed into the room.

"Listen, you three!" he roared, "either you tell me the truth about this lady or

I will boil each of you in oil!"

"But, sir, we already told you the truth!" we replied.

"The truth! You stubborn creatures, you don't know what the truth is! Enough of this nonsense! I have a huge kettle of oil boiling in the kitchen right now, just right to cook the three of you to a crisp! Francisco, what is this secret that lady told you?"

Poor Francisco trembled with fear. "I cannot tell you, sir."

The mayor grabbed my brother by the arm and rushed him out of the room. He slammed the door behind us. I gasped with horror! Francisco was to be boiled alive! I clung to Lúcia. We stood frozen to the floor, waiting to hear Francisco's screams as he was plunged in the boiling oil. But we heard nothing.

After several long moments, the door opened once more and the mayor strode in.

"That's one of you boiled. Now, my little Jacinta, it is your turn. Tell me this secret or you will be cooked too."

Huge tears ran down my face. "I cannot tell you the secret, sir. I can't, I can't," I sobbed in terror.

The mayor dragged me out of the room, just as he had done with my brother.

Lúcia was left alone. Again she stood there, listening for my screams, but none came. Oh, the fear that seized her! To be boiled alive in oil! She fell to her knees. "No matter what the mayor does to me, I cannot break

my promise to the lady. Please, good lady, help me to die bravely like Francisco and Jacinta, without a sound," she whispered.

Then the door opened. There stood the mayor once more, his eyes glinting.

"Your two cousins are cooked. Now will you talk?"

"No, sir."

The mayor grabbed Lúcia and hurried her off to the kitchen. She trembled in dread of what she would see there. As soon as the door was flung open, she stared in complete amazement. There we were, Francisco and I, very white but unharmed, sitting with the mayor's wife!

"There was no boiling oil," cried Francisco as he rushed to meet Lúcia. "He was only trying to frighten us."

"Yes," I said, close behind my brother. "He thought we would never be willing to die for the lady, but we were ready to do so. You were too, weren't you, Lúcia?"

As though in a dream, Lúcia nodded. Then she burst into tears of joy. "Oh, I was so frightened, but I would have died a thousand times rather than break our promise to the lady. She is so lovely, so kind, so good!"

The mayor was positively furious! He knew he would never get anything from us. He was obliged to admit defeat and sent us home.

# At the Cova on August 13

Our families were overjoyed to see us again! How relieved and happy we were to see them!

"But why didn't you come for us?" Lúcia asked her parents.

"Well, daughter," answered strict Dona Maria Rosa, "I thought you had been making up a story all along. So I thought, if these children are lying, it is the punishment they deserve. If they are telling the truth, Our Lady will watch over them."

Of course, they never expected the mayor to be so cruel. When we told them what he had done to us they were indignant.

After things had calmed down a little, my mother said with wonder in her voice, "In any case, I guess your lady did come."

"What do you mean?" we asked eagerly.

"Well, there was a huge crowd that day waiting for you to arrive. When you did not come they were angry and disappointed. But then, about twelve o'clock, there was a clap of thunder. Everyone was surprised since it was a clear day. Then, there was a flash of lightning so bright that it was clearly seen even with the sun shining. The sun then began to grow dim, and a beautiful glowing cloud settled on the holm oak, covering it completely. It remained there only a moment, then left. Everyone, astonished, knew something unusual had happened. They were no longer disappointed. Instead, they became furious when they heard you had been taken away."

"You see!" cried Lúcia, "The lady did come! She left because we were not there!"

"What a pity!" cried Francisco and I.

Yes, what a pity! To think that we missed her! And to think that she came and was disappointed!

# The Lady Comes

The next day, August 19, Lúcia, my brother, and another cousin were tending the sheep on a property called Valinhos. This place was much nearer to our village than the Cova.

"I wonder if we will have to wait until next month to see the Lady again," Francisco said sadly to Lúcia.

"I don't know. I wonder if there will be only five visits now instead of six," she said.

Suddenly, the air began to cool and the sun began to dim. Lúcia looked up.

"The lady! The lady is coming," she shouted. Then, turning to our other cousin she said, "Quickly, run home and tell Jacinta to hurry, for the lady is coming!"

There was a clap of thunder and a flash of lightning, and there stood the lady in a cloud of light atop another holm oak, slightly larger than the one at the Cova da Iria.

I arrived just in time, panting for breath. I was so happy to see her!

Lucia spoke first: "What does your Grace wish of me?"

"I want you to continue going to Cova da Iria on the thirteenth of each month and to continue praying the Rosary every day. In the last month I will work a miracle for all to believe." Then her face became more serious and even upset. "If they had not taken you to Ourem, the miracle would have been even greater."

Yes, she had seen everything from Heaven. She had seen what the mayor had done, and she had not liked it at all.

Then Lúcia asked her what we should do with the money that many people were leaving at the Cova for her. The lady said in her calm, heavenly voice, "Have two carriers for processions made. You, Jacinta and two other girls dressed in white should carry one of them. Let Francisco and three other boys carry the other. These shall be used on the feast day of Our Lady of the Rosary. The money that is left over should be used for the chapel that will be built later."

Then Lúcia asked for the cure of certain people. The lady answered that she would cure some during the year. Her face then became sadder and she said, "Pray, pray much, and make sacrifices for sinners. Many souls go to Hell because there is no one to sacrifice and pray for them."

Saying this, she began to rise toward the East.

After she left, Lúcia, Francisco, and I had the idea of cutting branches off the tree on which she had stood. Behold, the branches gave off a sweet, unknown fragrance! Everyone at home became aware of the scent.

# Francisco

The lady had asked us not to forget poor sinners. She mentioned them each time she came. By now, most of the people who came to Fátima truly believed that she appeared to us, and they were also praying many Rosaries as she had asked.

As for us, we continued to make our sacrifices. We still wore the coarse ropes around our waists. Lúcia and I thought all the time about sinners going to Hell forever, so we prayed and prayed very much for them. Francisco also prayed for them, but he thought more of how sad these sins made Jesus.

At times, he would leave our games, and we would find him crouched behind a wall or bush. "Francisco, what are you doing?" we would ask.

"I am thinking about the good God and how sad He is with so many people hurting Him. I want to console Him and keep Him company."

"Which do you like better," we asked, "praying for sinners or consoling the good God?"

"Consoling the good God. I want to console Jesus first and then convert men so that He won't be hurt anymore."

Another time we simply could not find him. We were getting very worried when Lúcia finally found him crouched behind a stone wall with his forehead touching the ground. She called him, but he did not answer. She had to shake him until he came to himself with a start, as if from a deep sleep.

"Were you praying?" she asked.

"I began to say the prayer of the Angel and then I started to think. I was thinking about God. I like to think about Him."

We noticed that he often kept his hand in his pocket. When we asked him what he was doing he would silently pull out his hand; he was holding his rosary. He preferred to pray the Rosary rather than play. "The lady said I have to say many Rosaries before I can go to Heaven, remember?" he would explain.

# The Fifth Visit

Twenty thousand people gathered at Cova da Iria on September 13. That was at least a hundred times the number of people living in our little village of Aljustrel! It looked like a human sea!

As the time approached for Our Lady to come, everyone noticed that the air suddenly cooled. The sun dimmed so much that even stars could be seen. Then another beautiful thing happened; a shower of glistening petals fell from the sky and

disappeared before touching the
ground. Suddenly, a brilliant globe was
seen moving slowly across the sky from
East to West. Then, the lady appeared.

　Again she told us to continue praying
the Rosary so the terrible war would end. She added that in October
Our Lord and Saint Joseph would come to bless the world. Then she
said most kindly, "God is pleased with your sacrifices, but He does not
want you to sleep with the ropes. Wear them only during the day."

　The ropes hurt so much that at times we could not sleep. Our Lord had seen this and was pleased, but He did not want us to lose our sleep.

Again Lúcia said that many people were asking for cures. The lady answered with endless patience, "Yes, I will cure some, others not. In October I will perform a miracle for all to believe."

Then she began to rise as she had done in the previous times. Everyone around us saw again the globe of light moving slowly through the sky. This time it moved from West to East. She had returned to Heaven.

# The Last Visit

The long-awaited October 13 finally came. That was the day of the great miracle. Many people crowded the Cova. We had great difficulty just getting to the holm oak.

We knelt, waiting once more. Now, everyone prayed the Rosary. We were eager to see the great miracle the lady had promised, but we were also sad. This would be the last time we would see her, at least for some time.

As we prayed, we saw the flash of lightning. We looked up to meet those motherly eyes looking kindly at us.

"What does Your Grace wish of me?" asked Lúcia.

"I wish to tell you that I want a chapel built here in my honor. I am the Lady of the Rosary. Continue to pray the Rosary every day. The war is going to end, and the soldiers will soon return to their homes," answered the Queen of Heaven. We already knew that the beautiful lady was none other than the Mother of God, but now she herself had said it.

Lúcia asked her again for the cure of some sick people and the conversion of others. The lady answered, "Some yes, others no. They must amend their lives and ask pardon for their sins." Her face then grew sadder and she said, "Let them offend Our Lord no more, for He is already greatly offended."

A marvelous thing then happened. As she began to rise, she opened her hands and sent the streaming light coming from them into the sun.

**"Look at the sun!"** Lúcia cried.

The day had been rainy, but now the clouds suddenly parted. Everyone saw the sun as a huge silver disk. It shone intensely. Then it began to dance, spinning like a gigantic ball of fire. Suddenly, it stopped. Its rim became scarlet and it started dancing again. Whirling through the sky, it scattered red flames all

around. This happened three times. Then the fiery globe began to tremble and shake, and then it plunged toward the terrified crowd, zigzagging horribly.

Some people screamed. Others prayed in a loud voice. All this lasted about ten minutes. Then suddenly, the sun zigzagged back to its place. It glowed distantly, as if nothing had ever happened. The crowd's rain-soaked clothes were totally dry.

While all this was happening with the sun, the three of us saw something else. Three scenes appeared beside the sun. Each represented the joyful, sorrowful, and glorious mysteries of the Rosary. Lúcia saw all three, but Francisco and I only saw the first scene.

The first was of the Holy Family; Saint Joseph appeared with the Child Jesus and Our Lady of the Rosary. Saint Joseph blessed the crowd, making the Sign of the Cross three times along with the Child Jesus.

In the second, Lúcia saw Our Lady of Sorrows, without the sword in her heart, and Jesus carrying the Cross on His way to Calvary. Jesus blessed the crowd.

Finally, Our Lady of Mount Carmel appeared crowned as Queen of Heaven and Earth. She held the Child Jesus near her heart.

With this, the miracle ended.

Now the lady would come no more. She had given the world a great message. She had asked people to pray, to do penance, and to stop offending Our Lord.

# School

A few weeks after the visits had ended, we began to go to school. It was hard for us because no one would leave us alone. They asked us all sorts of questions.

And then, there was Francisco. We noted that even though he tried, his mind was not on his books. Every chance he found, he would slip away to the village church to visit the Blessed Sacrament. He would sit there praying his rosary and keeping Our Lord company. He never forgot our Blessed Mother's promise that he and I would soon go to heaven. Nor did he forget that she had said he must pray many Rosaries. By now it was no longer hard for him to say the Rosary. He had learned to think of beautiful pictures for each ten Hail Marys. Shutting his eyes, he would think of a set of five pictures for each rosary. So, for example, for the first ten Hail Marys he would first think of the Archangel Gabriel as he appeared to the Virgin Mary. Then for the next ten Hail Marys he would think of the Blessed Virgin's visit to her cousin Saint Elizabeth, who was expecting Saint John. Then, he imagined the day the Baby Jesus was born in that poor stable in Bethlehem. He imagined the Blessed

Virgin Mary, Saint Joseph, the ox, the donkey and the three kings that had come to visit.....and so on.

With the autumn of 1918 came a terrible outbreak of the flu. My brother and I both fell sick. For the first two weeks, Francisco was extremely ill. When he improved a little, people began telling him how well he would soon be. But he only shook his head weakly and said, "I am never going to be well again. I am going to die."

"Nonsense!" cried his godmother. "I made a promise to the Blessed Mother that if you become well, I will sell as much of my wheat as equals your weight and give the money for her chapel at the Cova."

Again Francisco shook his head. "You won't have to keep that promise, Godmother, I know it."

# Our Lady Visits Again

During our sickness, the Lady of the Rosary visited us one day in our own home! She looked at us with unspeakable kindness and goodness! Our hearts glowed again with heavenly joy! Francisco was certain she had come to take him. But she said gently, "Not yet, Francisco. In a very short time I shall come and take you to heaven as I promised."

Then turning to me she asked, "As for you, Jacinta, are you willing to continue suffering and to convert still more poor sinners?"

I had wanted very much to go to heaven with my brother. But I only wanted to do what she wished. So I replied, "I will remain suffering as long as God wishes! I'll bring as many souls to Heaven as I can!"

She smiled. "Then you will suffer much. You will even go to a hospital. But you will accept everything to convert poor sinners and console the Immaculate Heart of Mary for the love of Jesus."

She then began to disappear.

# First Communion and Heaven

Before going to Heaven, Francisco wanted to receive Our Lord in Holy Communion. Even though he had not finished his Catechism, our parish priest decided he was ready to receive Jesus in the Host. Francisco asked Lúcia and me to help him prepare for his first confession. He wanted to remember absolutely everything he had ever done wrong. After confessing, he made his First Communion. When he received the Good Jesus in the Host, he was shining.

We asked, "Francisco, aren't you suffering anymore?"

"No," he replied, "the pain is gone."

Our Lord had taken away his pain while He was with him. We stayed and talked awhile about heaven. I asked him to greet Our Lord and Our Lady for me and to tell Them I was ready to suffer for sinners as much as They might wish.

"I will tell Them," he agreed.

Feeling tired, he wanted to sleep. When Lúcia and I left his room we heard the church bell toll. We looked at each other. We knew that someone else had died from the flu and wondered if Francisco would be next.

About six o'clock the next morning Francisco woke from a deep sleep. Raising himself in bed he pointed to the door and said with his eyes shining, "Oh! Look, Mother! Look at the beautiful light!"

"What light, son?"

"There, near the door. It's so beautiful!"

But his mother could not see anything. She helped settle him back in

his pillow and then left the room. His godmother entered. He stretched out his hands to her and said, "I am sorry for all the bad things I ever did, really and truly, Godmother."

She nodded kindly and sat by his bed. "Try to rest now," she whispered. "It is the only way to become strong and well."

But as she spoke, something in his face attracted her. He was so peaceful, so still... Francisco was now in heaven.

## My Journey

After my brother died, I became really sick. My parents decided to take me to a hospital in Ourem. But I did not want to go there! Ourem, was the same town where we had been put in jail! Lúcia helped me to think of Our Lady and the promise I had made to her to help save more poor sinners. So that gave me courage and I went.

I stayed two months in the hospital of Ourem, but my health did not improve. My parents brought me back home to Fátima. I began to think that Our Lady had changed her mind and that she might let me die at home. But, one day she appeared to me again and told me I would go to another hospital and that I would die there, alone.

One day, a famous doctor came to Fátima and visited our home to examine me. He told my parents that he knew of a very good surgeon in the great city of Lisbon. He would certainly make me better.

So, one day, my mother and I left for Lisbon. I knew I would never see my family and my home again. This thought made me cry. Lúcia knew it too, so we both offered Our Lady that great sacrifice.

In Lisbon I stayed at an orphanage run by nuns. There was one nun I especially liked. She was very good to me. I called her "Godmother."

She took care of me for two weeks before I went to the hospital for an operation.

The operation was not successful. Oh, how I suffered! How much pain I had all over! How far away I felt from my family and Lúcia! But Our Lady did not leave me. She came to visit me many times and encouraged me. One day Our Lady told me the day and the hour that she would come to take me to live in heaven forever.

On February 20, 1920, a good priest came to hear my confession. He thought I looked so well that he did not want to give me Communion. I offered God that last big sacrifice for poor sinners. I knew I would never receive Holy Communion again.

At 10:30 that night, the Lady of the Rosary came for me too.

# *EPILOGUE*

Ten years after Jacinta's death, the apparitions of Fatima were declared authentic by the Catholic Church. Devotion to Our Lady of the Rosary widely increased throughout the world. Today, in the spot where the Blessed Mother appeared, a chapel and a grand basilica now stand. Thousands of pilgrims flock to the shrine of Fatima every year to pray and to do penance as Our Lady asked. And from May to October, every night devotees come in procession in honor of Our Lady of Fatima.

The square becomes transformed into a sea of candles and voices are raised to Heaven in song and prayer. It is a very beautiful sight, and very moving. This, really, is the greatest miracle of all.

# America
# Needs Fatima

has an inspiring selection of devotion-building materials for adults and children.

For more copies of *Jacinta's Story* or for a complete listing of other titles, call **(717) 225-7147** or write:

**AMERICA NEEDS FATIMA**
**P.O. BOX 1868**
**YORK, PA 17405**

03D